THOUGHTS FROM THE WORLD'S GREAT RELIGIONS

Compiled and Edited
by O.P. Ghai

TOP OF THE MOUNTAIN PUBLISHING
Pinellas Park, Florida 34665-2244 U.S.A.

JUN '95

WI

TOP OF THE MOUNTAIN PUBLISHING
P.O. Box 2244
Pinellas Park, Florida 34665-2244
SAN 287-590X
FAX (813) 536-3681
PHONE (813) 530-0110

Copyright 1995 by
Top Of The Mountain Publishing

Library of Congress Cataloging in Publication Data
Thoughts from the World's Great Religions: a guide to the understanding of the fundamental unity underlying the twelve great living religions of the world/compiled and edited by O.P. Ghai.
p. cm.
ISBN 1-56087-048-6 (hardback): $21.95—
ISBN 1-56087-053-2 (pbk): $12.95
1. Religion—Quotations, maxims, etc. I. Ghai, O.P. (Om Prakash)
PN6084.R3T466 1995
200—dc20   94-8243 CIP

Cover and text design
by Powell Productions: Tag Powell and
Marcos A. Oliveira

Manufactured in the United States of America

JUN '95

Table of Contents

Preface

What is religion? For each individual, religion touches one's inner core belief, giving meaning to one's existence. Religious dogma, rules, and guidelines give substance to one's everyday behavior.

Of those who consciously choose a spiritual path on this plane of existence, there are hundreds of religions\myths\beliefs to incorporate. Of these religions, most may be traced to a basic twelve which have the most followers today.

O.P.Ghai has spent his life studying the scriptures, the holy words of the many prophets. Interpreting these sacred works is a unique adventure. In a couple of today's religions the sacred texts are copyrighted material and may not be reproduced without written permission—a legal technicality. Still in other religions, the message is so pure that in order to receive its message, it must be read in the original tongue in which it was written.

Please do not be offended if your specific religion is not included. We will be happy to work with the religious hierarchy for inclusion of your faith in the next edition of this book.

Treated separately from this text is information on Native American religions and African religions. Not suggesting they are inferior to the twelve religions described, this publishing house chose to print two in-depth studies of these past cultures, beliefs, and traditions in two separate books written by John J. Ollivier, *The Wisdom of Native American Mythology* and *The Wisdom of African Mythology*.

Please know it is not our intent to offend any believer, only to help in the understanding of one another. Here the author brings forth the thoughts, the underlying core beliefs of each of the twelve living religions. These are not just from the studies of O.P. Ghai, but from many religious scholars around the globe, who took their valuable time to read, augment, and support this work.

We are all people living in a world which is rapidly shrinking into a "global village." Yet, as we become more closely networked we strive to keep our identity, our precious hope that we are unique.

Multi-culturalism is on the rise, and we look to find how we are different not similar... for fear we will lose our identities. Most wars and skirmishes are ignited by fear over this identity crisis.

In this text, the crisis in religious identity is addressed. For here one will be able to identify with the underlying "Unity in Diversity."

This project is an act of love in the belief that each of us can make this a better world in which to live... when we accept our similarities.

Dr. Tag Powell
Publisher

A Reference in Time

In this book we will adopt designating time periods with "B.C.E." and "C.E." rather than B.C. (before Christ) and A.D. (*Anno Domini.* "in the year of the Lord"). It is more appropriate when writing about the *unity* in all religions, to indicate time periods Before the Common Era of Judaism and Christianity; and to use C.E. to denote time periods during the Common Era of Judaism and Christianity. Therefore the date 1200 B.C. is written in our book as 1200 B.C.E., and the year 622 A.D. is written 622 C.E.

Foreword

By his patient labor in collecting, collating and bringing together the wisdom of the twelve living religions, O.P. Ghai, the compiler of this anthology, has shown that the founding fathers of the faiths were not fanatics. Most of them emerged as opponents of barbarism and cruelty of their times, to reassert the truths of the previous prophets—truths which had often been debased, or fallen into disuse, or rejected by priests of one faith, merely because they were contained in the books of the other faiths with which they were in competition.

Mr. Ghai has followed the trend towards the freedom of men and women to think what they like. He is cannily aware that the perennial thoughts of the different faiths are similar though the words in which they are put are not the same. Take 'Anger,' for example:

One should not give way to anger, but should control it, says Buddhism.

God does not sanction anger, says Christianity.

One should so conduct himself as to avoid hatred or anger, says Confucianism.

Anger breeds confusion, says Hinduism.

Anger is not for the wise or the religious, says Jainism.

Love and not anger is commended, says Judaism.

Mr. Ghai has recalled similar sayings about Hatred, Love, Justice, Peace, and a number of other subjects.

While it is important to show the similarities in the basic wisdom of the faiths, we might keep in mind that this is being done to induce a mood of tolerant understanding in the new young and the old. It is from the point of view of positive history, for even when human relations change with adjustments in political and social systems, the freedom to think has been accepted, consciously or subconsciously, as the basic background of coexistence of peoples.

We must keep in mind the fact that an anthology like this, by revealing similarities of approaches to life, has to help the new young to build a far bigger consensus than that attempted by the faiths. The consensus is to save life itself (for which rules are made) from the threat of complete obliteration of all men and women with the deadliest of nuclear weapons.

This anthology is only one effort towards enlightenment, that humankind is kin.

We have to inaugurate a whole new literature in the school system, and in the school of life. It may inculcate the love of happiness in the here and now, which may invent such media as may inspire the will to change from aggressiveness to non-hurting; from fear and hate to free accepting; from patriarchal 'pedagogical poison' to free thinking— in fact to an education which may ultimately change human nature enough to allow survival of life into the 21st century and beyond.

Dr. Mulk Raj Anand
India

Acknowledgments

A special "thank you" to the following religion experts who have reviewed the manuscript and made suggestions:

Elizabeth Reis, S.S.J., D. Min., Sisters of St. Joseph, Nazareth, Michigan.

Allan C. Brownfeld, American Council for Judaism, Alexandria, Virginia.

Professor Cerif Mardin, School of International Studies of American University, Washington, DC.

Father John Ollivier, author of *The Wisdom of African Mythology* and *The Wisdom of Native-American Mythology*, Port Clinton, Ohio.

Rev. Frederick Potter, retired from the Board of the Council for a Parliament of the World's Religions. Cedar Lake, Indiana.

Ronald B. Precht, Baha'i Office of Public Information, Wilmette, Illinois.

Dr. K. C. Sheshagiri Rao, Dept. of Religious Studies, Cocke Hall of University of Virginia, Charlottesville, Virginia.

Mr. Rohinton Rivetna, President of Federation of Zoroastrian Association, Hinsdale, Illinois.

Dr. Tansukh J. Salgia, President, Bramhi Jain Society, Jain Organization Intn'l, Quincy, Illinois.

Dr. Rajwant Singh, Sikh religious leader, Silver Spring, Maryland.

Ms. Mary J. Stackhouse, Director of American Buddhist Shim-Gum Do Association, Brighton, Massachusetts.

Bishop Seigen H. Yamaoka, Buddhist Churches of America, San Francisco, California.

Mr. Elson Snow, Editor of the newsletter for Buddhist Churches of America, San Francisco, California.

H. Roy Kaplan, Ph. D., Executive Director of the National Conference of Christians and Jews, Tampa, Florida.

Introduction

There are twelve great living religions today. Under twenty-nine important topics including Love, Friendship, Duty, Courage, Faith, Hate, Happiness, Peace and Work, I have made a selection of sayings from the sacred writings of these religions. They reveal how religions, originating in very different cultures and in ages far apart, teach similar doctrines and similar principles of ethics and morals.

This humble compilation is not only an attempt to glean the best in living religious literatures, but is also a guide to the understanding of the fundamental similarity underlying the religions. I am sure it will provide comfort, guidance and inspiration to those who read it.

I have been a student of comparative religion for the last fifty years, but I have felt the necessity of publishing this small volume at this particular time when religious intolerance is at its height all over the world. If this attempt can bring sanity even to one religious fanatic bent upon harming his fellow beings simply because they believe in a different religion, I will feel amply rewarded.

O.P.Ghai

Dedication

This book is
a dedication to spiritual unity
in the face of religious diversity.
To the understanding that
all beings are created equal
in the mind of
Universal Spirit.

TWELVE
GREAT
LIVING
RELIGIONS
OF THE
WORLD

BAHA'I

The Baha'i religion is the most recent of the great religions. Its founder, Baha'u'llah (1817-1892 C.E.), was born in Persia (Iran) and in the end was banished to Akka in the Holy Land. He declared that the oneness of humankind is the new axis around which the spiritual and social life in an age of maturity revolves.

This concept includes three basic principles: the oneness of God; the oneness of the religions in their origin and goal, as well as the reconciliation between religion and science and their mutual cooperation in world unity; and the oneness of humanity. Baha'i is thus condemn all types of prejudice and advocate the equality of men and women. The Baha'i religion has about four million followers and is found in almost every country in the world.

BUDDHISM

The historical Buddha, Siddhartha Gautama (563-483 B.C.E.) was the son of a rich Hindu raja of the Sakya clan. The Buddhist teachings are based on Gautama's own experiences of "Enlightenment," which he gained after leaving his family to begin a spiritual quest. Buddha discovered three characteristics of existence: life is transitory, sorrowful and soulless. He gathered many disciples who followed his meditative discipline and formed a monastic and lay society. These people followed his teachings and adapted to moral rules and ethical behavior.

Nirvana, the goal for Buddhists, is a self-release (liberation) from Karma (the wheel of life-suffering, death, and rebirth) to the attainment of birthlessness and the quality of the peacefulness of ultimate reality, characterizing buddhahood. This is to be achieved through disciplined techniques of passionless detachment.

CHRISTIANITY

Christianity grew out of Judaism in the first century C.E., and developed into a religious movement during the Roman Empire. Christians claim many of the Jewish sacred writing as their own, and many editions of the *Bible* also include the books of the *Apocrypha*. The *New Testament* is the life, death and resurrection of their Messiah, Jesus of Nazareth, whom they believe died for their sins in order for them to be saved and enter the Kingdom of Heaven.

Jesus (the Christ), a Jew, steeped in Jewish tradition and culture, and his disciples broke away from the narrow nationalism and laws of the Judaism of the past to carry the high ethical idealism of the greatest of the prophets to all people, whether Jew or non-Jew.

Jesus' radical (at the time) teachings were that the Kingdom of Heaven was here; and that God was a loving, kind, gentle, and merciful One, not the vengeful, wrathful God of old. God forgave and accepted the sinner and saint alike.

CONFUCIONISM

China had been religious long before Confucius, who lived between 551 and 478 B.C.E. In fact, from its earliest days, about 2356 B.C.E., China has had an official religion. Confucianism is now the official religion of China. However, Confucius—latinization of K'ung Fu Tzw (Honored Philosopher K'ung)—its founder, thought of his work not as a religious text but as a social and administrative treatise during that time of government and moral decay.

The young Confucius became famous as a teacher, followed by his success in political office and then as an itinerant preacher. He believed that the wisdom of the past should be preserved and followed in the present. A main theme in his teachings were both obedience to elders while they were alive and veneration of their spirits after they were gone (ceremonies and rites). He stressed rightousness, loyalty, reciprocity, giving and receiving, as necessities in human relationships.

HINDUISM

Hinduism is the oldest living religion in the world, dating from about 2000 and 1500 B.C.E. From its beginnings to the present time, Hinduism has been changing and growing. The beliefs and doctrines of the early Hindus have undergone many changes with influences from its Vedic origins and the religions of Jainism and Buddhism, but there are some persistent themes throughout.

Hindus believe there are four goals or stages in life: (1) Duty, (2) Success, and (3) Pleasure through fulfillment; and (4) Release (negation) through knowledge, withdrawl (yoga and asceticism), and devotion to a god.

Hindus differ widely in their beliefs about theological matters while remaining Hindus all the same. Several attempts have been made to reform Hinduism. The reform movements spearheaded by a great many reformers have tried to relate the eternal truths to the changing times.

ISLAM

Islam is one of the world's most widespread religions, dating from the Hegira, or flight of the Prophet from Mecca in 622 C.E. Mohammed, its founder, was born in 570 C.E. at Mecca, the chief city of Arabia. He was called to be a prophet of God by Angel Gabriel who appeared to him on Mt. Hira.

The sacred writings of Islam is the *Qur'an (Koran)*. Islam (meaning submission) is based on what are known as the five pillars of Islam:

1. There is no God but Allah and Mohammed is His prophet.
2. Prayer, five times each day, facing Mecca.
3. Almsgiving for the poor and unfortunate.
4. A pilgrimage to Mecca once in a lifetime.
5. Fasting, especially during the Holy Month of Ramadan.

Mohammed's basic preaching was against worship of idols, polytheism, immorality and cruelty.

Followers of Mohammed are known as Muslims.

JAINISM

According to Jainism, there is no creator of the universe, because the universe matter was always here and will continue to exist, just as the creator could always have been here. So no particular deity is worshipped.

Instead, Jains pray to the Moksha, or liberated souls, who have infinite, absolute, and complete knowledge, vision, and strength. The Moksha inspire the Jains to their ultimate goal: ridding themselve of human form and thus, the shackles of *Karma*. The way to destroy old karma is to practice aceticism (voluntary depravation and suffering); the way to avoid new karma is to withdraw from all worldly involvement, as much as possible.

Jainism was the first organized effort to affect a reform of Hinduism (500-200 B.C.E.). The Jains are not opposed to any other religion and follow very specific dietary and behavioral codes. They follow five vows: 1) Noninjury (to humans and animals), 2) Nonlying, 3) Nonstealing, 4) Chastity, and 5) Nongrasping.

JUDAISM

Judaism is or the religion of the the Jews, sometimes called Israelites or Hebrews. They were led by Abraham, "the father of all nations," and Sarah from Ancient Mesopotamia to the Land of Cannaan, now known as Israel or Palestine (ca. 1800 or 1600 B.C.E.). The *Torah* (five of the law of the *Hebrew Scriptures*) given to Moses, recounts that God promised this land to them and their descendants forever. Abraham led his people from the belief in many gods to belief in one Almighty God.

The deepened call of the Jewish people came with the call of Moses, the Exodus of the Hebrews from Egypt in the 14th century B.C.E., and their renewal of their covenant with God in the Sinai desert. It was to Moses and this group that the *Ten Commandments* were given and a new covenant with God as God's choosen people: Isreal.

Judaism, in its long development from before 1200 B.C.E., has borrowed a great deal from other religions, but has also contributed greatly to many religious systems, particularly Christianity and Islam.

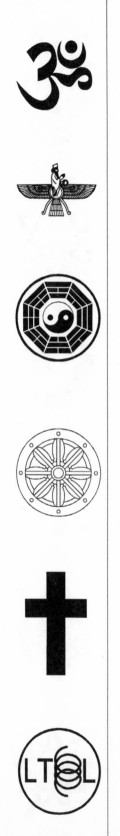

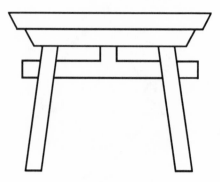

SHINTO

Shinto is the indigenous religion of Japan. All Japanese people are Shinto by nature of their birth. Unlike most religions discussed in this book, Shinto has no historical founder, no sacred scriptures, no strict dogmas. The term Shinto is Chinese in origin—*shen* (*kami* in Japanese) and *tao*—meaning "gods" or "spirits" and "way," respectively; thus "The Way of the Gods." One of the basic beliefs in Shinto is the idea that all gods or spirits, all people, and nature itself were born from the same parents. Because of this, all things—seen and unseen—have a divine nature, including ancestral spirits and natural phenomena.

According to some authorities, Shintoism unquestionably represents the distinctive religious genius of Japan from the beginning influence of Chinese Buddhism about the sixth century C.E. Others argue that it is in no sense a religion but is rather a patriotic cult. Whether we call it a religion or not, it has definitely made a significant contribution to the political theory and national stability of Japan.

SIKHISM

Sikhism is among the most modern of the great living religions. Its founder, Guru Nanak, lived between 1469 and 1538 C.E. in the province of Punjab in India.

After an intese religious awakening, Nanak, a Hindu Vaishnava, began a life of teaching through poetry and song. His religion still adhered to the Hindu beliefs in karma and transmigration, but he rejected the Hindu caste system and the Muslim circumcision because these were "physical" marks which separated worshippers of the same God into warring groups. Sikhism was originally intended to bring unity.

In his verses, Nanak used many terms for God: the Creator, the Compassionate, the Self-Existent; the True, the Only Real; and *Govind, Hari, and Ram.*

Though it has a small number of adherents and was founded during modern times, Sikhism has exerted considerable influence upon the religious life of the East.

TAOISM

Taoism (pronounced "Dowism"), the oldest of the personally-founded religions of China, is one of the "Three Religions" of that vast land, with the other two being Confucianism and Buddhism. The first book expressing Taoist ideas (*Tao* meaning "way") was probably written between the sixth and fourth centuries B.C.E. It is uncertain as to the author of the book—some believe the information is from an old philosopher named Lao Tzu. (The book does advise against seeking fame or praise from one's successes.) Taoism scorned Confucionism and advocated a natural, effortless way of living (non-striving and non-action).

There are many who maintain that Taoism should not be classed as a religion at all. Others point out that it was originally simply a way of ethical living and was not organized as a religion until late in its history, close to the beginning of the Christian era.

ZOROASTRIANISM

The history of Zoroastrianism reveals that it has had a profound influence over other religions, particularly Christianity. Today its followers are scattered throughout the Middle East, India, Pakistan, Europe and North America. A great many of the concepts found both in the *Old* and in the *New Testament* stem directly from Zoroastrianism, though the religion itself is not mentioned anywhere in the *Bible*.

Zarathushtra (known as Zoroaster in Greek literature) was one of the earliest prophets to preach monotheism.

Zoroastrianism is a "reflective" religion, not dogmatic, not prescriptive. Do good or bad and reap the consequences—there is no blind obedience prescribed. Zarthushtra's views were that man not only has the freedom to choose between good and evil, but also the responsibility to actively promote good, vanquish evil, and move himself and the world toward the final resurrection, a date of perfection and ever-lasting bliss.

ANGER

ANGER

BAHA'I
Never become angry with one another... Love the creatures for the sake of God and not for themselves. You will never become angry or impatient if you love them for the sake of God.

BUDDHISM
He who controls anger has power far greater than those who give way to it. The one is master of his emotion while the other is mastered by it. Hatred is damaging to humankind and should be eliminated.

CHRISTIANITY
God does not sanction anger. One should be slow to anger and always ready to forgive. If we hate our "brother" or "sister" we are like murderers. The mark of a Christian is love, not hatred.

CONFUCIANISM
One should so conduct himself as to avoid hatred or anger from others. Mild speech and demanding little of others are ways to avoid their anger.

HINDUISM
Anger breeds confusion. He who would be clear and unconfused must avoid anger.

ISLAM
Abu Huraira reported God's messenger as saying: "The strong man is not the good wrestler; the strong man is only he who controls himself when he is angry.

ANGER

JAINISM
Love and not anger, is commended. Anger causes strife and destruction. One should respond to anger in others with love and kindness. That way he will turn away the anger of others. Only fools give way to anger.

JUDAISM
Anger is not for the wise or the religious. They will endure persecution and not be angry. Only the ignorant and the sinful will give way to anger.

SIKHISM
Avarice is a dog, Falsehood a sweeper, Cheating is the eating of a dead body. Slander is the dirt that my tongue tastes, and Anger is the fire that burns me as at cremation; I indulge in nothing but self-esteem. See, these are my doings, O Lord.

TAOISM
No one should be angry with holy men since they are not angry with anyone. Return anger with goodness. Do good to those who hate you.

ZOROASTRIANISM
Never give way to the deadly emotions of Anger, Envy, Fear, and Grief; sublime them with good thoughts, words, and deeds.

BROTHERHOOD

BROTHERHOOD

BAHA'I
It beseemth all men, in this Day, to take firm hold on the Most Great Name, and to establish the unity of all mankind. There is no place to flee to, no refuge that anyone can seek, except Him.

BUDDHISM
A friend is a great treasure and he should be cherished as a brother. One should make good men his closest friends, his brothers.

CHRISTIANITY
All people are brothers and sisters. If we have anything against our brother or sister, we should make peace with them before attending to other religious duties. As one treats a brother or sister, so does he treat God. To hate one another is evil. Love should rule the world.

CONFUCIANISM
Friendship and brotherhood are cardinal virtues. One should gather about many friends and should love them as brothers. The wise man will choose friends worthy of brotherly love.

HINDUISM
The good man does not discriminate between friend and foe, brother and stranger, but regards them all with impartiality. A true friend will be sympathetic to you at all times.

ISLAM
All mankind is one family, one people. All men are brothers and should live as such. The Lord loves those who so live.

BROTHERHOOD

JAINISM

Be fair and impartial to all. Treat all men as brothers at all times. As one treats men, so should he treat all animals. They are also our brothers.

JUDAISM

God has made all people brothers and sisters, and they should live together in peace at all times. It is good for us to act in unity. Such action will be blessed by God and will prosper.

SHINTO

Heaven is the father and earth the mother of all men. Therefore, all men are brothers and should dwell together as such. By so living, the country will be free from hate and sorrow.

SIKHISM

Get together, my brethren, and remove all misunderstandings through regard for each other.

TAOISM

The spirit of brotherhood, kindness, is necessary if one would win friends. The spirit of the market, where men sell goods, should not be the spirit of the good man.

ZOROASTRIANISM

One's friends should be righteous (truthful) people. A righteous man will radiate truth to all his friends.

COURAGE

COURAGE

BAHA'I
The source of courage and power is the promotion of the Word of God, and steadfastness in His Love.

BUDDHISM
The wise man is not afraid. He knows his strength and does not fear. Likewise, he knows his weaknesses and does not attempt the impossible.

CHRISTIANITY
God is strong, the helper of the good. Therefore, we should not fear, but face life with courage and confidence that the source of all power in the universe is on our side. God watches over even the weakest of people.

CONFUCIANISM
The man of principle is courageous. He knows the right and will fight for it at all costs. God is on his side, and he takes courage from the knowledge of this fact.

HINDUISM
To realize that God is all and all is God gives man courage. He does not shrink.

ISLAM
God will guide the good. Therefore they shall have no fear. He will lead them through all the rough spots of life.

COURAGE

JAINISM
A man may conquer thousands and thousands of invincible foes but that is of no real consequence; his greatest victory is when he conquers his own self through indomitable courage.

JUDAISM
Be courageous, for God will not fail you. If the Lord is on the side of the righteous one, whom then shall he fear! God will give you the strength you need when the time arrives for it.

SIKHISM
Brave is he, who possessing strength displays it not, and lives in humble ways. He is brave, who fights for the downtrodden.

TAOISM
The philosopher is not influenced by praise or blame. He knows the truth and is not afraid, regardless of what happens to him in this world.

ZOROASTRIANISM
Courage begets strength by actively fighting evil that is manifested by bad thoughts, bad words and bad deeds. Courage grows from fighting danger and overcoming obstacles. Develop the courage to act according to your righteous convictions, to speak what is true, and to do what is right.

DEEDS

DEEDS

BAHA'I
It behooves each one of you to manifest the attributes of God, and to exemplify by your deeds and words the signs of His righteousness, His power and His glory.

BUDDHISM
Deeds determine one's place in society. One becomes an outcast or a highly-placed person by his deeds. Evil deeds are easy to do; good deeds are difficult; but the good deeds pay the highest rewards.

CHRISTIANITY
People are known by their deeds, and are judged even so by God. God will reward good deeds and punish evil ones. To profess goodness is of no value; one must do good deeds or be condemned.

CONFUCIANISM
Reward will follow every good deed. Only by doing good deeds can a man know the true joy of living and have a long life.

HINDUISM
One becomes what one does. The doer of good deeds will become good, and the doer of evil deeds will become evil. Action, the doing of the good, is superior to renunciation. Thus, at all times one should be doing good.

DEEDS

ISLAM
On the Day of Judgment every soul shall be judged in accordance with his deeds. To do good drives out evil.

JAINISM
The good show the way to others by their good acts. Each day passes never to return. Therefore, do good at all times, for you can never call back a day to perform a good deed that was not done.

JUDAISM
Do good at all times, for man will be judged by his works.

SIKHISM
Man's deeds are recorded by the Divine. One becomes good in the eyes of the Divine by doing good deeds. God is the zenith of good.

ZOROASTRIANISM
We come to the Wise One through good thoughts, good words, and good deeds. One should not be content with good thoughts and good words, but to also do good deeds for the benefit of the world.

DUTY

DUTY

BAHA'I
That one indeed is a man who, today, dedicates himself to the service of the entire human race.

BUDDHISM
One should be faithful to his duty at all times regardless of the situation. Faithfulness to duty brings the greatest of rewards.

CHRISTIANITY
One has a duty to God and duties toward others. One should take care to discharge one's duties. It is one's duty at all times to do the will of God.

CONFUCIANISM
Man's duty comes from Heaven. Therefore, he fails in his duty at his peril. The wise man makes duty his aim at all times.

HINDUISM
Never falter in doing your duty. God has decreed man's duty, and to fail in one's duty is to disobey God. It is through duty that a man reaches perfection.

ISLAM
All men who do their duty will receive a fitting reward from the Lord.

DUTY

JAINISM
A wise man discovers his duty and does it at all costs. It is the duty of all to be impartial and to abstain from causing injury to any living being.

JUDAISM
The whole duty of people is to fear God and keep God's commandments. This involves love and service to God with one's whole heart.

SHINTO
The path of duty is near at hand, men seek it in what is remote.

SIKHISM
He alone is a householder who disciplines his sense desires; begs from God contemplation, austerity and self-control; and gives in charity all he can by earning through the labor of his body.

TAOISM
The middle way is the duty of man. He should avoid all excess. In this way he fulfills his duty toward man and God.

ZOROASTRIANISM
One has to be prompt in performing one's duties.

EVIL

EVIL

BAHA'I

The source of all evil is for man to turn away from his Lord and to set his heart on things ungodly. In all matters, moderation is desirable. If a thing is carried to excess, it will prove a source of evil.

BUDDHISM

Evil actions will be punished inevitably, and good actions rewarded with happiness. The good man will loathe evil at all times and will keep himself pure.

CHRISTIANITY

Christians will hate evil and will keep themselves free even from the appearance of evil. To know what is good and not to do it, is sin.

CONFUCIANISM

Heaven visits punishment or happiness upon man in accordance with his good or evil acts. The rewards of goodness are inevitable, just as are the punishments of evil.

HINDUISM

He who is evil cannot hope to attain eternal happiness. Heaven punishes the evil. All pain and suffering comes from evil-doing.

JAINISM

Avoid all evil. One may commit evil by doing something wrong or by approving another's evil act. Do not cause others to sin.

EVIL

JUDAISM

Evil is the cause of suffering. Everyone is evil and must repent. God will reward those who flee from evil and seek the good. God is always ready to pardon.

SHINTO

After three years, an evil becomes a habit, a necessity. See no evil, hear no evil, speak no evil.

SIKHISM

When the clothes are soiled and rendered impure, they are cleansed with soap. When the mind is defiled by sin, it is rendered pure by the love of his Name. Call them the evil spirits, who are engrossed in Maya, lust, anger, and pride. Call him an evil spirit who does evil actions, and knows not the Master. Remove sin from your heart, and serve others. By remembering God, all your sins shall be washed off.

TAOISM

Those who do evil in the open light of day—men will punish them. Those who do evil in secret—God will punish them. Who fears both man and God, he is fit to walk alone.

ZOROASTRIANISM

When a man makes an honest effort to cleanse himself day by day of his evil thoughts, evil words, and evil deeds—then will follow in their wake, as the day the night, good thoughts, good words, and good deeds.

FAITH

FAITH

BAHA'I
The essence of faith is fewness of words and abundance of deeds; he whose words exceed his deeds, know verily his death is better than his life.

BUDDHISM
Faith is necessary for the virtuous life. One's faith will not go unrewarded. Prosperity follows upon faith.

CHRISTIANITY
Faith is necessary, but it must be accompanied by works. One who is faithful even to death will receive a crown of life. One who asks in perfect faith shall receive. Faith is basic to full understanding. But faith without good works is dead.

CONFUCIANISM
He who lacks faith will not succeed. One must hold to faith at all times. Heaven makes great demands upon one's faith, but God is with man and he should never waver in his faith.

HINDUISM
Faith is the pathway to wisdom. This faith will come if one yearns in his heart for it. The most prized of God is the man of faith.

ISLAM
Man should have faith in God, for God will always prove faithful. But God has no patience with the unfaithful.

FAITH

JAINISM
The man of faith has chosen the right pathway. He should practice his faith at all times.

JUDAISM
God is faithful and will preserve the faithful. The person of faith can expect great rewards from God.

SHINTO
Even the slightest yielding to doubt is a departing from the nature of man. Faith is fundamental to human beings.

SIKHISM
Good life and immortality are the rewards of the faithful. The religion of the Wise One will cleanse the faithful from all sin.

TAOISM
To have less than enough faith is to have no faith at all. The Divine will repay faith with faith and faithlessness with faithlessness.

ZOROASTRIANISM
Faith is not to be dogmatic. Everyone has to cultivate his inner-conscience to judge what is right and wrong, and then follow what is right.

FAMILY

FAMILY

BAHA'I
If love and agreement are manifest in a single family, that family will advance, become illumined and spiritual.

BUDDHISM
The aged should be respected and revered. He who does this will receive great rewards and will prosper. Children should give support to their parents. Always honor your parents.

CHRISTIANITY
Children must respect and obey their parents, but the parents must also respect their children. There is to be mutual understanding and appreciation within the family.

CONFUCIANISM
Filial piety is highly respected. The virtuous man will never neglect his parents. Love and respect for relations and elders is the beginning of love and respect for all members of the state.

HINDUISM
Love and respect must reign in the home. This is commended because every member of the household is a soul, and as a soul he is worthy of love and respect. Faithfulness must mark the relationship of husband and wife.

FAMILY

ISLAM
A child should be grateful both to God and to his parents. The family is a unit, and should beseech God as one.

JAINISM
The child should support his parents when he is able to do so. Although the family should work together to aid each other, each one must suffer for his own deeds. One's family is of no use to him at the time of judgment. Then he shall be judged in accordance with his individual deeds.

JUDAISM
Family love and solidarity is basic to Jewish life. Children must honor and respect their parents and obey them at all times. The parents must teach children and rear them in the ways of the Lord.

SIKHISM
Son, why do you quarrel with your father, due to him you have grown to this age. It is a sin to argue with him. Always look up to the Highest, living among your kith and kin, like the lotus that stands above its roots which are in mud.

ZOROASTRIANISM
Obedience, peace, charity, humility, truth, and righteousness should prevail in every home. May God give us, and our children, good intellect so we become obedient.

FORGIVENESS

FORGIVENESS

BAHA'I
When the sinner finds himself wholly detached and freed from all save God, he should beg forgiveness and pardon from Him. Confession of sins and transgressions before human beings is not permissible, as it hath never been nor will ever be conducive to Divine forgiveness. Moreover, such confession before people results in one's humiliation and abasement, and God—exalted be His glory—wishes not the humiliation of His servants.

BUDDHISM
Whatsoever may be the cause of your suffering, do not wound another, forgive him.

CHRISTIANITY
We should be forgiving. As we forgive our fellow beings so God will forgive us. God is forgiving and is ready and anxious to forgive those who ask for His forgiveness.

CONFUCIANISM
One should forgive if the act is unintentional, but should punish the intended evil act.

HINDUISM
God will forgive the sinner, if he earnestly casts away his sin. Human forgiveness is the way to happiness among men. A wise man will always be ready to forgive.

FORGIVENESS

ISLAM

God loves those who forgive their fellow beings. God is forgiving and is anxious to forgive all those who will come to Him with contrite hearts.

JAINISM

I forgive all the living beings. All living beings may forgive me. I cherish friendly feelings towards all. I do not hold any ill-will towards man, beast, or plant.

JUDAISM

The Lord forgives all sins. God is forgiving at all times, if the wicked ones will forsake their ways.

SHINTO

Forgive others but yourself never.

SIKHISM

Countless people have perished, without the spirit of forgiveness. Remove malice from your own heart, and behold! the whole world is your friend.

ZOROASTRIANISM

Enemies and bad persons are to be won over by good words and not by violence.

FRIENDS

FRIENDS

BAHA'I

It is incumbent upon everyone to show the utmost love... and sincere kindliness unto all the peoples and kindred of the world, be they friends or strangers.

BUDDHISM

One should pick one's associates from among the wise and the good. Evil associates will corrupt a man. A man who reproves intelligently should be sought out since his words are the advice one needs.

CHRISTIANITY

Evil companions corrupt good morals. Shun those who are not good. Wise people will seek out those who will help them to become better and attain greater sanctity. Shun the idle and the unproductive and seek out the industrious and the creative.

CONFUCIANISM

Seek out the company of those who can give good advice and whose example is good. One may be friendly to all men, but one should be discriminating in one's choice of associates. Good associates will do you good, therefore cling to the best.

HINDUISM

Look upon all the living beings as your bosom friends, for in all of them there resides one soul. All are but a part of that Universal Soul. A person who believes that all are his soul-mates and loves them all alike, never feels lonely.

FRIENDS

ISLAM
Avoid those who do wrong. To associate with the wicked is to cast suspicion upon oneself. Therefore, avoid such suspicion by seeking out only the good men as associates.

JAINISM
Do not allow yourself to be deluded by evil associates. Make friends with those who are considerate both towards other people and toward animals.

JUDAISM
Do not follow the path of the wicked, or associate with those who are evil. Good friends are best.

SIKHISM
Friend, if you possess some good, let us be friends. Let us be partners for doing good, and let us ignore each other's flaws.

ZOROASTRIANISM
The good should associate with those whom they can help. A virtuous man will radiate his virtue far and wide. One is fortunate to be the associate of such a good man.

GIVING

GIVING

BAHA'I
To give and to be generous are attributes of Mine; well is with him that adorns himself with My virtues.

BUDDHISM
Liberality is a virtue. The wise and good man will share what he has with others. In this way he will save himself. Giving is saving.

CHRISTIANITY
One should give to all who ask, for in giving to the needy one gives to God. Christians should bear the burdens of others and should share their goods with those in need. The Lord loves a cheerful giver.

CONFUCIANISM
Benevolence is a characteristic of the wise. The superior man gives generously to the needy. He knows that this is the chief element in humanity.

HINDUISM
Giving with cheerfulness is the way to security and happiness. Giving is superior to receiving since the giver acquires a friend and protects himself from enemies. The wise man will always share with others.

ISLAM
The pious man will give alms. His gifts will return to him. God loves the giver. As God has been generous to man, so should man be generous to his fellow beings.

GIVING

JAINISM
Charity without fellow-feeling is like sowing a fallow land.

JUDAISM
Those who have should give to those who have not. The poor should always be helped. One who gives to the poor gives to the Lord. If one does not give when the poor ask, one will not be aided when one is in need.

SHINTO
Be generous to all creatures, both human and animal. Long life is the reward for generous giving.

SIKHISM
Only what one gives to others will be preserved for him in the future world. The generous will find contentment.

TAOISM
One should help all those who are in need, and should not think of his reward. The good will be frugal in order to be liberal to those in need.

ZOROASTRIANISM
The Wise One is generous. So should all His followers be generous. For one who helps the poor and is generous is the most welcome guest of God.

GOLDEN RULE

GOLDEN RULE

BAHA'I
The principle of fairness, often called the Golden Rule, is common to all religions. Baha'u'llah has reemphasized this spiritual law in this way: "Lay not on any soul a load which ye would not wish to be laid upon you, and desire not for any one the things ye would not desire for yourselves. This is My best counsel unto you, did ye but observe it."

BUDDHISM
Hurt not others in ways that you yourself would find hurtful.

CHRISTIANITY
Remember that you are like other men. As you fear and suffer, so do they. Therefore, do not do those things which will cause them trouble. As you would not harm yourself, do not harm others. Do unto others as you would have them do unto you. One should love his neighbor as himself.

CONFUCIANISM
What we do not like to have done to ourselves, we should not do to others. The rule of philanthropy is to draw one's self a parallel for the treatment of others.

HINDUISM
Behave with others as you would with yourself.

GOLDEN RULE

ISLAM

Anas told that when God's messenger said: "Help your brother whether he is acting wrongfully or is wronged," a man asked, "Messenger of God, I help him when he is wronged, but how can I help him when he is acting wrongfully?" He replied: "You can prevent him from acting wrongfully. That is your help to him." No one is a believer until he desires for his brother that which he desires for himself.

JAINISM

One should treat all beings as he himself would be treated. Since all beings hate pain, he should kill nothing.

JUDAISM

What you hate, do to no one. We should love our neighbor as ourselves.

SIKHISM

As you sow, so shall you reap; this [earthly] body is the result of your actions.

ZOROASTRIANISM

Do not do unto others all that which is not well for yourself. Preach not by mouth but by acts of service.

GUIDANCE

GUIDANCE

BAHA'I

Religion confers upon man eternal life and guides his footsteps in the world of morality. It opens the doors of unending happiness...

BUDDHISM

Trust in the Lord and He will guide you right. One who has this trust need fear nothing. He can be at perfect peace and happiness, for he will be guided right.

CHRISTIANITY

If we trust in God, we will be carried through all hardship and troubles. One should have complete confidence in God. Even in persecution we should not falter, for God will guide us to our reward.

CONFUCIANISM

God is with the good man. Therefore, he should never fear. God will guide the good right. Follow the will of God without questioning, for it is true and the end will be success.

HINDUISM

No enemies can overcome the believer; he trusts in God, and knows that God will guide him through all troubles.

ISLAM

The Lord has created and will guide man through life. Those who trust in His guidance at all times will find that the Lord will not fail them.

GUIDANCE

JAINISM

From the roots grows up the trunk of the tree, from the trunk shoot up the branches, out of them grow the twigs and the leaves; and then there are produced flowers, fruits, and juice. Similarly, obedience to the guidance of Jina is the root of the tree of religion, and the liberation is the highest resultant (juice). It is through His guidance that one achieves immortal renown and abiding peace.

JUDAISM

Trust in God at all times. God will lead you even through the shadows of death and will protect you in the presence of your enemies.

SIKHISM

Be not led astray by the illusion of the world, (and know then that) without the Guru, no one is ferried across (the sea of existence). The Guru shows the Path to the strayers. Sing then the Lord's praise, for, this alone is thy eternal duty.

ZOROASTRIANISM

God is our protector and guide. In Him must we trust and never waver. He is all powerful and will never fail those who yield to His guiding.

HAPPINESS

HAPPINESS

BAHA'I
Happy are they who understand; happy is the man that hath clung unto the truth, detached from all that is in the heavens and all that is on earth!

BUDDHISM
The wise and good man will be happy in this world and in the next. He has the secret of perfect contentment and joy. One should not seek after happiness, but should find it as a natural result of good deeds.

CHRISTIANITY
The Christian life is a happy one. Despite persecution and tribulations, the Christian is happy because he has right on his side and his reward will be great in heaven.

CONFUCIANISM
Even in the most meager of circumstances, the man who lives rightly will be happy. Ill-gotten gains will never bring happiness. Heaven grants happiness to the good.

HINDUISM
True happiness comes not from external things, but through attachment to things spiritual. It is an inner joy which nothing outside can destroy. It comes from God and is a reward for goodness. Only the wise have real happiness.

ISLAM
Happiness will come when one turns to God and seeks union with Him. The good will be rewarded greatly for their works and will be happy.

HAPPINESS

JAINISM

Happiness comes through self-control. The man who is able to subdue himself will find happiness in this and in the next world.

JUDAISM

Judaism is joyous. Those who have the Lord on their side should be happy, rejoicing all the time. Happiness results from good works. If people keep the Law, they shall be happy.

SHINTO

Virtue goes hand in hand with happiness.

SIKHISM

We shall find happiness in the worship of the Lord. He made everything and is the source of all true happiness.

TAOISM

Human happiness comes from perfect harmony with one's fellow beings. The source of divine happiness is complete accord with God. The good shall be truly happy.

ZOROASTRIANISM

Righteousness is the source of true happiness. Only those who live truthfully shall know happiness. The unrighteous man shall bring misery.

BAHA'I
Blessed are such as hold fast to the cord of kindliness and tender mercy, and are free from animosity and hatred.

BUDDHISM
Hatred is damaging to humankind. One who gives way to hatred is no longer master of himself.

CHRISTIANITY
Love and not hatred should rule. If we have any hatred in our hearts, we should cast it out before turning to our religious observances. To hate is to be a murderer.

CONFUCIANISM
Those who speak harshly will stir up hatred. One should demand much of himself and little of others. By so doing one will avoid hatred.

HINDUISM
Hatred breeds confusion. Clear thinking and careful action can come only when the heart is free from hatred.

ISLAM
Abu Ayyub al-Ansari reported God's messenger as saying: "It is not allowable for a man to keep apart from his brother more than three days, the one turning away and the other turning away when they meet. The better of the two is the one who is the first to give a greeting."

HATE

JAINISM
Hatred will drag down the soul and defile it. To attain purity of soul, one should avoid hatred at all costs.

JUDAISM
It is wrong to hate a brother or a sister. Hatred begets strife, and strife destroys a people. Only the fool will give way to hatred.

SIKHISM
He whose mind is imbued with the One alone feels not jealous of another.

TAOISM
Return goodness for hatred. The wise man hates not, but seeks always to do good. He will not enter a dispute and thus can have no one disputing and hating him.

HOME

HOME

BAHA'I

My home is the home of peace. My home is the home of joy and delight. My home is the home of laughter and exultation. Whosoever enters through the portals of this home must go out with gladsome heart. This is the home of light; whosoever enters here must become illumined.

BUDDHISM

The home should be a place of mutual understanding and love, of chastity and faithfulness, of reverence for the aged and respect for the young. There should be no selfishness among members of the family.

CHRISTIANITY

In the home the children should honor the father and mother, and the parents should respect the children. The parents' duty is to teach the children and rear them in the truly religious life.

CONFUCIANISM

The home, with its atmosphere of love and respect, should be the model for the entire world. At all times, affection, harmony, and honor, should reign in the home. Filial piety, begun in the home, extends to the state and becomes devotion to the ruler.

HINDUISM

The highest law of the home is fidelity among its members. The wife should be faithful, the children obedient, and the father understanding and industrious. Thus will develop the perfect home.

HOME

ISLAM
Prayer should dominate the home. In it the parents and children should serve the Lord at all times. The home is a unit and should approach the Lord as one. Here kindness to parents should dominate the children, and the parents should see to it that the children are nurtured rightly in all religious matters.

JAINISM
The child should support his father and mother when he is able to do so and they are in need. But, in religious matters, the man must stand alone.

JUDAISM
The home should be a place of worship. Here all members should serve the Lord and honor and respect should reign. The home in which righteousness rules will stand against the world, and the children going out from it shall prosper and receive bounteous rewards.

SIKHISM
Yea, such a householder is Pure, like Ganga's water.

ZOROASTRIANISM
The home should be a place where obedience, peace, love, generosity, humility, truth, and righteousness reign. Here children will respect their parents. To such a home will come contentment, knowledge, prosperity, and glory.

IMMORTALITY

IMMORTALITY

BAHA'I

It is evident that the loftiest mansions in the Realm of Immortality have been ordained as the habitation of them that have truly believed in God and in His signs. Death can never invade that holy seat. Thus have we entrusted thee with the signs of thy Lord, that thou may persevere in thy love for Him, and be of them that comprehend this truth.

BUDDHISM

The good and wise will find happiness in the life to come. The evil and thoughtless will die eternally. Heaven is a place of bliss for the good. Here one who has lived earnestly and wisely shall find his reward.

CHRISTIANITY

God has prepared a home after death for the good. All here on earth changes and passes away, but the one who obeys the will of God lives forever. Heaven is a place of rewards and hell a place of punishment. Each person shall receive justice after death.

HINDUISM

The soul withdraws from the earthly body in order to make for itself a new and more beautiful body. The wise man will become immortal. Death is the taking off of the robe of life to put on the robe of immortality. The good and just shall live forever.

ISLAM

The good, and those who have died in the service of the Lord, shall be rewarded with eternal life. God will gather all his faithful followers to Himself after death. Theirs is the reward of Paradise.

IMMORTALITY

JAINISM

The ultimate goal of human life is to liberate the soul from the bondage of karma (good and bad) through total renunciation of desires of greed, passion, hate, love, etc. Thus, the soul evolves into perfection. The cycle of birth, death, and suffering ends forever. Human form is the highest form of life, once it achieves perfection, it can become like God.

JUDAISM

The dust will return to dust, and the spirit of a person will go to its everlasting home. The Lord will reward the good with eternal life and the spirit will dwell forever with God who made it.

SIKHISM

The good man dies only to go home. He does not die, but lives forever. Heaven is the company of the saints.

TAOISM

Death is a going home. The good and wise shall suffer no harm even though the body dies.

ZOROASTRIANISM

He who lives this life in accordance with Truth shall have bliss in this life and immorality in the life beyond.

JUSTICE

BAHA'I

O Son of Spirit! The best beloved of all things in My sight is Justice; turn not away therefrom if thou desires Me, and neglect it not that I may confide in thee. By its aid thou shalt see with thine own eyes and not through the eyes of others, and shalt know of thine own knowledge and not through the knowledge of thy neighbor. Ponder this in thy heart; how it behooves thee to be. Verily justice is My gift to thee and the sign of My loving kindness. Set it then before thine eyes.

BUDDHISM

The wise man will weigh matters carefully so that he may judge justly. Hasty judgment shows a man to be a fool.

CHRISTIANITY

All judgments should be made justly. Beware lest you fall into evil judgments. God is just and will judge all people justly, according to their deeds.

CONFUCIANISM

The man of honor desires justice and will seek after it in all his actions. Only the fool is unjust.

HINDUISM

The one who hurts pious men falls victim to his own designs. This is Divine justice.

ISLAM

Live a just and honest life. God does not do injustice, and He expects His followers to be just. Act justly at all times and under all conditions.

JUSTICE

JAINISM

God, let me not stray away from the path of justice. I may remain ever steadfast against the denunciation by others; should ever be unmindful of the prospects of immediate death or life through millenniums, keeping my equanimity in poverty and plenty.

JUDAISM

The Lord loves justice and has erected God's throne upon it. The one who deals justly with all people at all times shall truly live.

SHINTO

Injustice shall be overcome by justice. If one has made a promise, he must fulfill it justly even though it be made with the unrighteous. Man should think and act justly at all times.

SIKHISM

Our acts, right and wrong, / At Thy Court shall come to judgment; / Some be seated near Thy seat, / Some ever kept distant; / The toils have ended of those, / That have worshipped Thee; / O Nanak, their faces are lit with joyful radiance, / And many others they set free. / We are saved not, / If thou judge according to our actions, / Forgive us, O Thou Forgiver of all, / And lead Nanak across this ocean of life.

ZOROASTRIANISM

One should be just to friends and foes.

LOVE

BAHA'I
In the world of existence there is no greater power than the power of love.

BUDDHISM
One act of pure love in saving life is greater than spending the whole of one's time in religious offerings to the gods, sacrificing elephants and horses.

CHRISTIANITY
Love is supreme in Christianity. It is the heart of religion. God's love for us and our love for God, the love of each of us for one another, and the love of the Christian for all others are central themes of Christian teaching.

CONFUCIANISM
Love makes a spot beautiful; who chooses not to dwell in love, has he got wisdom? Love is the high nobility of Heaven, the peaceful home of man. To lack love, when nothing hinders us, is to lack wisdom. Lack of love and wisdom lead to lack of courtesy and right and without these man is a slave.

HINDUISM
The Lord is the lover of all beings, but He especially loves those who keep His laws and are devoted to Him. One can best worship the Lord through love.

ISLAM
Abu Dharr said: God's messenger came out to us and said: "Do you know which action is dearest to God most high?" When one man suggested prayer and Sakat and another Jihad, the Prophet said: "The action dearest to God most high is love for God's sake."

LOVE

JAINISM
One should show compassion to all creatures and obey the Law at all times.

JUDAISM
One should love God with all one's heart, with all one's soul, with all one's mind, and with all one's strength. And one should love their neighbor. The stranger has a claim on one's love. God loves the good person, the righteous. God also loves the sinner and seeks to draw people from their sin and to Himself.

SHINTO
The Lord will visit the home where love reigns. Love is the representative of the Lord.

SIKHISM
One who loves God truly will be cleansed of all his impurities. We obtain salvation by loving our fellow beings and God.

TAOISM
God's love is for the good man at all times. The Wise One taught universal love toward one's fellow beings and His followers should follow His teaching.

ZOROASTRIANISM
Everyone should love truth. A truthful man is the beloved of the Lord and should love Him and be a friend to Him in return.

MAN

MAN

BAHA'I
Man is the supreme Talisman. Lack of a proper education hath, however, deprived him of that which he doth inherently possess.

BUDDHISM
Man is the product of his thinking. All that he is, all his ideals, likes and dislikes, his very self, is the result of thought.

CHRISTIANITY
Humans are a little lower than the angels. We are the measure of all values. It is for us that the world was created and for us Jesus came to earth and died. We are God's workmen on earth. If we fail, all fails.

CONFUCIANISM
Heaven has made man good. His original nature is good, but many depart from it. The earthly in man pulls him down and away from Heaven. Those who follow the heavenly part of themselves are great, while those who follow the earthly part are evil.

HINDUISM
Man is the highest of animals. He is an animal with an immortal soul which cannot be hurt by the world. There is nothing nobler than humanity.

ISLAM
God created man to sit on His throne on earth. Man is God's viceroy on earth.

MAN

JAINISM

Due to his karmas or deeds, each soul is caught in the vicious cycle of birth and death, and revolves in the four life forms of hell, heaven, animal, and human. Human form is the only form of life which can control its senses and through rigorous discipline, take the soul to the journey of perfection, total bliss.

JUDAISM

Most people are enamored of pleasure and do not reach the moral heights possible for humanity. The self is the foe to greatness and is as dangerous as pride, anger, and greed. The self is to be subdued.

SIKHISM

Man's body is the dwelling place of God. God is the soul of man, his eternal nature.

TAOISM

Man is both human and divine. The divine in him is eternal and of infinite worth. The human may pass away, but the Divine is everlasting. His goodness comes from God.

ZOROASTRIANISM

The mind of man enclosed in a body comes from the Divine. Thus, man should serve only the good and flee from all that is wicked. The man who does better than good is like unto Thee, O'Ahura.

MEDITATION

MEDITATION

BAHA'I
Meditation is the key for opening the doors of mysteries. In that state man abstracts himself; in that state man withdraws himself from all outside objects; in that subjective mood he is immersed in the ocean of spiritual life and can unfold the secrets of things-in-themselves.

BUDDHISM
Great are the rewards of contemplation. One who trains himself in the art of meditation will penetrate the heart of truth and discover great spiritual riches.

CHRISTIANITY
Thinking on the great things of life results in greatness. If one would be good, one must contemplate the good. All virtues will be strengthened by meditation upon them. This, too, is the way to clearer understanding.

CONFUCIANISM
One should avoid bad, evil thoughts. One should at all times think that which is good. Careful consideration of the end as well as the beginning and the middle will save one much trouble.

HINDUISM
Those who do not meditate can have neither steadiness nor peace. The great and the wise meditate constantly on the divine. This is source of strength and the way to knowledge of the Supreme One.

MEDITATION

ISLAM
Meditate upon God and you will find peace. Meditation must be in humility and constant if one would reap its true rewards.

JAINISM
Contemplation is the means of obtaining stability of mind. Even though one is severely persecuted, one must obey the law of silent meditation.

JUDAISM
Meditation brings understanding. One should contemplate God in all His greatness at all time. This is enjoyable and brings the greatest peace and happiness. To meditate upon the Law of the Lord is the duty of all believers.

SIKHISM
Just as there is fragrance in the flower, and re-flection in the mirror, similarly, God lives within; search Him in thy heart, O brother.

TAOISM
To a mind that is "still" the whole universe surrenders.

ZOROASTRIANISM
Keep the plan and purposes of the Lord always in mind. Meditate upon them day and night. Then you will come to clear understanding. When one is in doubt his piety will help him choose right.

OBEDIENCE

OBEDIENCE

BAHA'I

O son of man! Were thou to speed through the immensity of space and traverse the expanse of heaven, yet thou wouldst find no rest save in submission to Our command and humbleness before Our Face.

BUDDHISM

Those who obey the law and follow studiously the commandments shall have serenity of mind, joy, and prosperity. Obedience is the way to the good things of this life and of the life to come.

CHRISTIANITY

True Christians are known by the fact that they obey the commandments of God. If we desire true life here and hereafter, we should keep the commandments. The Christian will obey God at all times rather than humans. If we keep God's commandments, God will dwell in us and act through us.

CONFUCIANISM

To obtain the favor of Heaven, one should observe all the statutes of Heaven. Those who reverently observe these statutes and are obedient to the will of Heaven shall have happiness and shall become men superior.

HINDUISM

The laws of God are eternal, lofty, and deep. The man who is obedient to them will be happy and, after death, will experience joy unsurpassable.

OBEDIENCE

ISLAM

All shall be well with the believer who hears the word of the Lord and obeys. The law of the Lord has been set down for man to read and obey. The punishment for disobedience is severe.

JAINISM

The fool refuses to obey the Law and is sorry when he reaches the hour of death. Man is created to fulfill the law of God. The wise and pious are always obedient to the law of God.

JUDAISM

The commandments of the Lord are just and should be obeyed. To disobey God will result in punishment, to obey will result in happiness and blessedness. God will show no mercy to those people or nations who refuse to obey.

SIKHISM

Man is to God what a servant is to his master. Thus, he should obey at all times. If man obeys he will have honor and happiness and will eventually meet his Master.

TAOISM

The complete and perfect man is the one who obeys the will of the Lord at all times.

ZOROASTRIANISM

The Lord is wise. Thus, all His exhortations are good for His followers and His commandments are best for humankind. Immortality is the reward He offers to the obedient.

PEACE

PEACE

BAHA'I

Today there is no greater glory for man than that of service in the cause of the 'Most Great Peace.' Peace is light whereas war is darkness. Peace is life; war is death. Peace is guidance; war is error. Peace is the foundation of God; war is a satanic institution. Peace is the illumination of the world of humanity; war is the destroyer of human foundations.

BUDDHISM

True happiness comes to those who live at peace with their fellow beings. The aim of all should be to learn peace and live peacefully with all men.

CHRISTIANITY

Jesus is the Prince of Peace. He came to this earth to bring peace to all people. The peacemaker is blessed and shall be a child of God. We should seek the way of peace and finally come to peace with God.

CONFUCIANISM

Seek to live in harmony with all your neighbors and at peace with thy brethren. Peace and love should reign throughout the world. The Most High God seeks peace among His people.

HINDUISM

If one would find happiness and security, one must seek peace. The peaceful mind will become established in wisdom. God is a god of peace and desires peace for all people.

ISLAM

God will guide men to peace. If they will heed Him, He will lead them from the darkness of war to the light of peace.

PEACE

JAINISM
The enlightened will make peace the foundation of their lives. All men should live in peace with their fellow beings. This is the Lord's desire.

JUDAISM
Judaism looks forward to an ideal time when peace shall reign throughout the world. God commends peace and urges all His followers to work for peace. The peaceful life offers the greatest opportunity for happiness and prosperity.

SHINTO
The earth shall be free from trouble and men shall live at peace under the protection of the Divine.

SIKHISM
The *Sat Nam* [True Name] is my support; it is my food and drink; by it my hunger of every kind is satisfied. By saturating my mind, it has satisfied all my longings, and given me peace and happiness.

TAOISM
The wise esteem peace and quiet above all else. The good ruler seeks peace and not war, and he rules by persuasion rather than by force.

ZOROASTRIANISM
Humankind should mutually love one another and live in peace as brothers and sisters, bound by the indestructible hand of Humanity.

REPENTANCE

BAHA'I

Beseech thou the One true God that He may enable everyone to repent and return unto Him. So long as one's nature yields unto evil passions, crime and transgression will prevail.

BUDDHISM

Whatever faults one may have, one should confess them and seek forgiveness. Confession is a necessary part of repentance.

CHRISTIANITY

All people are sinners. Therefore, they should repent, confess their sins, and seek forgiveness of God who is ready always to forgive those who are truly repentant.

CONFUCIANISM

Whenever a person is in the wrong, he should hasten to confess his error and make amends.

HINDUISM

To the extent that one has sinned, one should confess and earnestly beg God's forgiveness and mercy. If one does this, God will hasten to forgive and wipe away one's sins.

REPENTANCE

ISLAM
The Lord is quick to forgive those who confess their sins and turn to Him for forgiveness. One who has sinned should seek the Lord with a repentant heart. He will surely find mercy.

JAINISM
Repent of pleasures and instruct others to do so. If one lives only for the present, and does not prepare for the future, one will repent later on.

JUDAISM
If we hide our sin and do not confess it, we shall not prosper. God is willing and anxious to forgive the ones who confess their guilt and truly repent.

SIKHISM
Relinquish your sins and have recourse to good actions. Repent if you have committed any sin.

ZOROASTRIANISM
If one has made a confession of his sins and does earnestly resolve to do numerous good deeds for each wrong deed, then the wrong doings will be out-weighed. The religion of the Wise One teaches to deliver the untruth (wrong) into the hands of the truth (right).

SINCERITY

BAHA'I

Honesty, virtue, wisdom, and a saintly character contribute to the exaltation of man, while dishonesty, imposture, ignorance, and hypocrisy lead to his abasement.

BUDDHISM

Be not slothful or flippant, but be earnest at all times. Goodness comes from earnestness. God loves the earnest, sincere man.

CHRISTIANITY

One's religious actions should not be for showing but should be done in earnestness. At all times the true Christian is sincere and earnest. A Christian is never the hypocrite who acts merely for show.

CONFUCIANISM

Whatever you do, you should do with all your heart. Heaven will help the man who is sincere, and one's fellow man will trust him if he is sincere and earnest.

HINDUISM

The Lord does not favor those who are not sincere and honest.

ISLAM

God is not to be fooled. He knows whether or not a man is earnest in his professions and will deal with all men according to this knowledge. One who repents in earnestness will be forgiven.

SINCERITY

JAINISM
Clear thinking comes through sincere and earnest effort. One can be proficient in religious practices only to the degree that one is earnest and sincere. Through sincere actions one becomes pure.

JUDAISM
The Lord will help those who are earnest. God is near to the sincere and knows our inner being. God is not fooled by outward appearances.

SHINTO
Sincerity is the single virtue that binds divinity and man in one.

SIKHISM
To pretend religion is of no avail. Earnestness is the only basis for true religious acts.

TAOISM
The manner of Heaven is earnestness. If one is sincere and earnest in one's acts, one will attain to the truest sainthood.

ZOROASTRIANISM
As long as a man is earnest, his reward will be great.

WAR

BAHA'I

When a thought of war comes, oppose it by a stronger thought of peace. A thought of hatred must be destroyed by a more powerful thought of love. Thoughts of war bring destruction to all harmony, well-being, restfulness, and content.

BUDDHISM

Intentional killing of any living being is condemned. Peace, and not war, is the ideal and should be sought by all who are truly religious.

CHRISTIANITY

The peacemakers, and not the war-makers, are blessed. Those who take the sword shall perish by the sword. War is the road to destruction, while peace is the road to happiness and prosperity.

CONFUCIANISM

God desires peace, not war. Everyone should strive to dwell in peace with his fellows. The man subdued by force is in his heart still rebellious, but one who is won by love will be loyal forever.

HINDUISM

Causing injury to any creature is wrong. The wise man will seek always to avoid strife and will dwell in peace. The ideal for life here on earth is peace, not war. No one should seek to extend his power through war.

ISLAM

Peace is to be sought by all. If there is war the religious man will seek to establish peace. The Lord has ordained peace, and no one can engage in war without endangering the stability of the world.

WAR

JAINISM
Never kill anything for any reason whatsoever. The wise live at peace with all men, whatever the cost. War is totally condemned.

JUDAISM
Only fools give way to war. The wise seek peace. The peace-loving, the meek, shall inherit the earth. The Lord will judge between nations, and wars are of no avail.

SHINTO
Let the land under heaven enjoy peace and be free from war. The Sun-Goddess will protect the country so that it may live at peace.

SIKHISM
When all efforts to restore peace prove useless and no words avail, lawful is the flash of steel then, and right it is the sword to hail.

TAOISM
War is always followed by disastrous years. He who truly serves as a ruler of men will not lead his nation into war. Arms are unblessed and are full of sorrow.

ZOROASTRIANISM
Where there is conflict try to bring peace.

WEALTH

BAHA'I

The essence of wealth is love of Me; whosoever loves Me is the possessor of all things, and he that loves Me not is indeed of the poor and needy. This is that which the Finger of Glory and Splendor hath revealed.

BUDDHISM

Wisdom and self-mastery are true wealth. Material possessions are not real wealth, for they can be taken away from a man. Real wealth is everlasting.

CHRISTIANITY

Moth and rust will corrupt earthly treasures. Therefore, real treasures are heavenly, where nothing can destroy them. One's heart will be with one's treasures. Therefore, turn from mammon to God. Do not count the wealth of this world as valuable. The only true value lies in spiritual wealth.

CONFUCIANISM

Prosperity comes from Heaven. Wealth gained by unrighteousness will not last. The only true wealth is that which comes through right acting. Too often riches are accompanied by pride and other evils.

HINDUISM

One should work constantly and seek after wealth. But, if one gains wealth, one should share it with those in need. Beware lest wealth shut the door on the good life. Riches are but means to doing good and should not become the goal of life.

WEALTH

ISLAM

Wealth should be employed at all times for the things of the Lord. He who wastes his wealth in evil actions is condemned. Wealth must not be allowed to turn one from service to God.

JAINISM

Wealth is fleeting and will never completely satisfy anyone. To put faith in wealth is to be a fool, for it will cause pain both in this world and in the next.

JUDAISM

Trust not in wealth. It is fleeting and may be the cause of much evil and suffering. The poverty of a good person is more to be prized than the wealth of the evil one. If one has wealth, one should use it for good and not for evil.

SIKHISM

In prosperity many come and surround a man. When fortune frowns at him, all abandon him and no one comes near. Of what use is wealth, amassed by wrongful means?

TAOISM

One's person is of more value than all one's wealth. Therefore, one with wealth must beware lest one sacrifice oneself for his wealth. Riches acquired unjustly will become poison to the soul.

ZOROASTRIANISM

Prosperity and wealth are the rewards of right living and come from the Wise Lord. Thus, wealth must be employed in the service of the Lord.

WORK

WORK

BAHA'I

It is enjoined upon everyone of you to engage in some form of occupation, such as crafts, trades, and the like. We have graciously exalted your engagement in such work to the rank of worship unto God, the True One.

BUDDHISM

Works, and not birth, determine one's place in the world. At all times one should work diligently and with earnestness. Hard work is praised.

CHRISTIANITY

God works and so we should work. The Christian will be diligent in good works all the time, for a person is to be judged by their works. As we work for the good, it is God who works in and through us.

CONFUCIANISM

Not ease, but work is the mark of a good man. The superior individual does not indulge in luxurious ease, but works constantly for the good. He is superior in that he does things which the base cannot understand or appreciate.

HINDUISM

One becomes what one does. The man who does good becomes good, and the man who does evil becomes evil. The motive of one's works should not be the consequences. One should do good despite the results. No one who does good will come to an evil end.

WORK

ISLAM
Everyone should strive to excel in good works. Work constantly. God will observe your works and judge you according to whether they are good or evil.

JAINISM
A day once gone will never return. Therefore, one should be diligent each moment to do good. We reach the goal of the good life by pious works.

JUDAISM
God will judge each person according to works. All shall be known by their works. Whatever one undertakes to do, one should do it with all one's might. God commands us to work and promises that He will be with us in all good works.

SIKHISM
God has determined from the beginning the works man must do. No man can escape this determination. Men become saints or sinners by their works only, not by their professions. Good works bring men to a clear knowledge of the Divine.

ZOROASTRIANISM
We come to the Divine through our good works. Thus, at all times man should strive to work well so that he may gain recognition in the eyes of the Wise Lord. The perverted man who gives up work does not attain any good.

WRATH

WRATH

BAHA'I

If a man exercises his anger and wrath against the bloodthirsty tyrants who are like ferocious beasts, it is very praiseworthy; but if he does not use these qualities in a right way they are blameworthy.

BUDDHISM

A true disciple is free from all passion, including wrath. To give way to wrath is to bind oneself to a master who will destroy. Happiness lies in freedom from wrath.

CHRISTIANITY

Everyone should beware of wrath. Do not become angry without cause. Love, and not anger, is the mark of a true Christian. Put away all wrath and malice and seek to dwell in friendliness with all people. When a man slaps you, turn the other cheek.

CONFUCIANISM

Do not deal with your fellow beings as though you were superior to them. Those who do will find themselves hated. To avoid the wrath of others, demand little of them and much of yourself.

HINDUISM

Wrath breeds confusion. One who would be master of himself and of all situations must avoid wrath. The ideal is to live free from hate and anger.

ISLAM

Abu Huraira told that a man asked the Prophet to give him some instruction and he said: "Do not be angry." The man repeated that several times and he replied: "Do not be angry."

WRATH

JAINISM
Wrath is a passion which defiles the soul. The wise man will avoid wrath lest he be caught in the toils of passion as a fly is caught in glue. Even though he is beaten, the religious will not give way to wrath.

JUDAISM
Wise people are slow to wrath. They give soft answers and thereby turn away wrath on the part of others. Love, and not wrath, should be the goal of all true believers, for wrath leads to strife.

SIKHISM
Wrath is the cup, filled with worldly love, and pride is the server. Through excessive drinking in the company of falsehood and avarice, the mortal is ruined.

TAOISM
Return goodness for hatred. Do not become angry and do not quarrel with your fellow beings. The wise man is free from wrath at all times.

ZOROASTRIANISM
Wrath and jealousy are the creed of evil ones. Wrath is to be suppressed, violence is to be guarded against by all who wish to prosper.

About the Author

Shri O.P. Ghai (1919 - 1992) was an author of experience. His many works on the *Qur'an, Japji* and the *Bible* testify to not only his linguistic ability, but also his spiritual leanings, both of which are essential for a translation of these texts used in this book.

O.P. Ghai was known for his speaking and communication abilities. He traveled widely in his homeland of India, and abroad, addressing seminars and conventions on educational and cultural themes. His rich experiences of life, and as a teacher and writer, led him to found and edit "Sharing," a journal devoted to successful living and the Indian book industry. Throughout his life he believed individuals have the power to shape their destiny as well as the destiny of society.

A publisher by profession and a believer by faith in the fundamental unity underlying the great living religions of the world, he sought to promote religious co-existence through the written as well as the spoken word.

Imbued with a deep religious sense, Mr. Ghai had a lifelong, reverent devotion to the study of the various scriptures. He selected from each of the great living religions a passage which seemed to capture essential messages.

The selections carry with them a high degree of subjectivity, but Mr. Ghai has done the selections with such finesse that the borderline between subjectivity and objectivity has virtually disappeared. Given the size of the book, one could hardly have done better. The English rendering is superb,which ensures the smooth flow of the selected passages. Ghai created the perfect guide book for the growing number of English-speaking readers looking for a volume which will tell them the essential messages of the great living religions in one sitting.

Bibliography

Major sacred writings of the
World's Great Religions some from which
selections have been made.

BAHA'I

Gleanings from the writings of Baha'u'llah
in Kitab-i-Aqdas (The Most Holy Book)
Writings of Baha'u'llah - A Compilation
Selections from the writings of 'Abdu'l-Baha'

BUDDHISM

The Dhammapada
The Vinaya Pitaka
The Sutta Pitaka

CHRISTIANITY

The Apocrypha
The New Testament

CONFUCIANISM

The Chung Yung (The Doctrines of the Mean)
The I Ching (Book of Changes)
The Lun Y (The Analects)
The Meng-Tge (The Book of Mercius)
The Shih Ching (The Book of Songs)
The Shu Ching (The Book of History)
The Ta Hs eh (The Great Leaning)

HINDUISM

The Bhagavad Gita
The Dharmashastras
The Rig-Veda
The Upanishads

ISLAM

The Qur'an (Koran)

JAINISM

The Ayaranya Sutra
The Sutrakritanga
The Uttaradhyayana Sutra

JUDAISM

The Hebrew Bible
The Hebrew Scriptures
The Mishnah
The Torah
The Talmud

SHINTO

The Kojiki
Selected Materials

SIKHISM

Asa DiWar
The Guru Granth
The Japji
The Rahiras

TAOISM

The Tao Te Ching
(The Book of the Way and its Virtues)
The Writings of Chuang Tzu

ZOROASTRIANISM

The Yashts
The Yasna
The Vendidad
The Visperad

Index